MY LETTERS
AND
OTHER TIDBITS

Never forget your dreams!
M. K. Ehlers

Acknowledgements

I wish to acknowledge several who have helped bring me to this point in getting my first book in print.

My oldest granddaughter, Debra, has been my inspiration since she published her first book a few months ago so I decided if she could do it, so could I.

Two of my daughters, Marie and Katherine have listened to me for years about writing and have suffered being asked to critique or proof read pages and pages.

My granddaughter, Amanda, has helped me with learning how modern day technology works and has taught me much.

My grandson, Johnathon, has also assisted me with technology and is the subject for some of my poetry.

PREFACE

As far back as I can recall, I have written: stories, poetry, beginnings of books, anything I could put on paper. Being an author has been a dream since childhood and although I have set that dream aside during years of making a living and raising children, it has never waned. I am confident many people grew tired of listening to me talk about my books in progress (there have been several).

I sincerely hope I find readers who enjoy my efforts.

In the year 2000, I was forced to give up my employment due to an injury. Sitting home was boring so I wrote the following poem. I called it

The Not Working Blues
I woke up this morning and stretched, oh......so slow.
Something's just not right; I'm feeling so low.
For hours and hours, I've been in my bed.
I've slept, turned, rolled, watched tv and read.
I'm cool. I'm chilled. I'm freezing. I'm hot.
Hours of rest and together I'm not.

There's some kind of problem and if I had to choose.
I'd guess it's a case of the not working blues.

My dishes are clean. My table is clear.
No dust, bugs or fuzzies to be found in here.
With time on my hands and minutes to spare
I opened my windows to let in some air.
I've tinted my tresses and mud masked my face.
Sewed on some buttons and mended some lace.
Even with things spruced up, this façade's a big ruse.
It's clear I'm suffering from the not working blues.

I've typed my life story and read lots of others.
I've written to aunts, uncles, cousins, sisters and brothers.
Read the Well Street Journal and The New York Times.
I've pondered the comparison of apples, oranges and limes.
My paints and brushes which had been packed away
Waiting 'till I could find a more convenient day
Were unpacked and tried and tried and tried.
That latent talent I dreamed of --alas—has vanished. I cried.

My face is pale.
My mind's gone stale.
I need to get into my coat and shoes.
I'm sure my problem is the not working blues.

So, even though I realized that not working was dulling my life, it still took me 15 years to find the courage to put my writing out for the world to see.

This is a true story but some of it has been written in a sort of 'tongue-in-cheek' style in an effort to insert a bit of humor so it will be interesting enough to keep the reader interested.

PART I

MY LETTERS AND OTHER TIDBITS

I AM

I was a seed.

I grew.

Now, I speak.

I sing.

I whisper.

I read.

I write.

I lead.

I follow.

I listen.

I hear.

I ponder.

I advise.

I AM.

As stated in the preface, this is an attempt to tell the story of a busy and fruitful life. And, what a life it has been. I have attempted to describe its highs points in *MY LETTERS*.

Many of you probably thought you would be reading letters I have written or received over my lifetime. Sorry to disappoint you, but not one such letter is to be found in this tale. Instead, you will be regaled with a different kind of letters......my letters, the letters following my name and letters that denote who I am and what I am and what I have done with my life during the seventy-eight years of my existence.

During my years of employment, I attended several seminars and noticed most of the speakers had impressive letters after their names, designating their field of expertise. Some in the audience chuckled as we tried to decide what some of them meant. As we shared dinner one night, we wondered if we could be those speakers if only we had some of those designations.

A few weeks later as I was driving to my next seminar, thoughts of those letters were still tickling the edge of my brain. I decided I did have some important letters but the need to get checked into the hotel room and grab a snack before the first meeting left little time to dwell on them.

After a great dinner served in one of the hotel's conference rooms while the schedule was being announced followed by a relaxing dip in the pool, my mind still had not strayed from thoughts of my letters. Years of living and working have earned me several titles and I have heard myself given a few titles by various acquaintances but shall omit some in an effort to not offend any reader.

Pen and paper in hand, I wandered into the lobby for a bit of soothing music provided by a realistic looking mannequin poised believable over piano keys. Music to think by, I thought, and started on my notes. An hour later, this story was clearly in mind. My letters were just as impressive and as numerous as any of those speakers. I was on my way to being Myra Enders, VFA. (Very Famous Author) This designation however, probably belongs at the end of the story after this book has become world recognized. But, being last makes it no less important than any others I realized I had earned.

O.O.E.K.
(ONE OF EIGHT KIDS)

What a life! Only someone raised in a large family could even begin to understand the workings in the life of eight siblings: love, hate, envy, support, jealousy, protectiveness, competition, pride, hope, No need to go on. Every possible emotion known was stretched to the limit. As much as physical appearances differed, so did our interests. Timing had some influence in this aspect of our personalities due to years between our births and birth order. I consider myself fortunate to have been born in the middle of this group so that I was influenced by both older and younger brothers and sisters. We were born two years apart except for one time when it was three years. .We range in age from 69 to 84 although three have died. Being one of eight kids was a great way to start life.

P.W.
PERFECT WIFE

Perfect? Of course! Aren't we all? I had thirty-four years to perfect my claim of being the perfect wife. Every night, my husband was met by a freshly showered, sexily attired temptress who had just finished running the vacuum and setting the dining table with china and crystal on a linen table cloth and napkins. A tasty dinner would be warming in the oven awaiting the arrival of the 'king of the castle'. The king's after dinner ritual was propping slipper-clad feet up while watching his favorite detective show on TV. This gave me time to clean up the kitchen, supervise children's baths, pack tomorrow's school lunches and freshen up for a night of cuddling, *if* I could stay awake that long. Oh yes! Being Myra Enders, perfect wife, provided me with an opportunity to excel in a variety of fields.

M.E.
MOTHER EXTROIDANAIRE

S.M.
SUPER MOM

These two impressive designations are so intertwined as to be almost inseparable. As much as I enjoyed being a mother (and occasionally, the wife part) it is easy for a woman to be lost behind the faces of the different roles she plays. Depending on the day and time, a mom may be a super chef, a maintenance person, a tutor, chauffeur, or a cleaning woman. I have, in fact, served as more than one of those positions at the same time.

Picture if you will—while the man of the house is leisurely having a second cup of coffee (after all, he has a busy day ahead) I am struggling to pull boots on in preparation for a mad dash to the car during a heavy downpour which turns out to be a little heavy for rain—more like sleet or snow. Having intended moving the car as close as possible to the kitchen door, so "Miss Junior Class Princess" can keep her hair dry, I now have to scrape the windows. I am shivering and icicles decorate my hair.

After dropping children at two different schools dropping off dry cleaning, picking up milk and bread I still have an hour or so left before I have to leave for work. I might even get to have a cup of tea and a glance at the headlines of the daily paper which I have not actually read in weeks.

But never mind my lack of R and R. I am fulfilling society's expectations of successfully being a M.E. and S.M.

W.L.S.
WOMAN LACKING SOMETHING

Probably ninety percent of the women reading this can identify with this title. Lacking? It is difficult to put a finger on just what is lacking. Could it be a lack of recognition for such an enormous responsibility? Could it be *society's lack of respect for a person who might aptly* be called a jack of all trades? Could it be a resentment of being called things like "the old lady"? The little woman. Ah, yes. Just the way women want to be thought of, or at least men seem to think so. Nothing little about the responsibilities that take up a wife and mother's time. Nothing womanly about some of the chores it is assumed "the little woman" enjoys. Can anyone really be so dense as to believe women actually enjoy dipping into dirty water and mopping up muddy footprints and Kool-Aid spots smeared by dog paws?

Can a man really think the little woman finds pleasure in picking up dirty underwear where he stepped out of them or smelly socks to be pulled out of pant legs?

Children are too young to understand that God didn't create mothers as slaves for them. Their needs and wants are uppermost in their minds and with Mr. Macho as an example, mothers fall prey to being depended on for things which other family members are capable of doing.

Never let it be said that I did not enjoy the role of mother, even enjoyed 'doing' for them. When, however, is the line drawn between giving one's services and giving one's self over to obscurity? How proud I have been to see my children go to school dressed in the best I could afford even though I may have been wearing last century's fashions. I recall one time, probably in the 60s or 70s, one of the hottest fashions was a hip length front opening vest usually worn over a long sleeved blouse and slacks or skirt. Probably every woman in my office has one or two and I wanted one but could not afford one nor did I really need one. Usually, my wardrobe took back seat in my priorities but this time, I just HAD to have one. Flash! My solution, at the time, seemed like a flash of brilliance. By trimming one-thirds of the length off a too small jumper, cutting it down the front and using a few inches of facing tape, I had one of those vests. The sewing skills I learned in Home Economics classes in high school came in handy. Undoubtedly it did not look as fashionable as I hoped at the time. But I could walk into the office and feel like I was living in the right century.

How many nights I sat up checking homework, trying to make sure *my* children got top grades. Perhaps my dreams of going to college could be sated by being involved in school work. Sort of vicarious learning?

Somehow checking math from a dog-eared book sticky with bubble gum just wasn't the same as opening a new college level geometry text while looking at an actual, professional adult.

Husbands and children, except age, are very much alike—

"Where's my red tie dear?"

"Didn't you wash my blue shirt Mom?"

"Hey Mom, will you iron my jeans?"

Of course, I have nothing better to do. While they are devouring the breakfast I cooked for them, why was it my duty to do their last minute necessities?

Finally, everyone is out of the house except me and I am alone with just enough time to gulp down a few bites and get dressed for my job and put the ingredients for beef stew in the crock pot and load the dishwasher and feed the cat and, and, and…You get the idea. The problem though is that this scenario was set years ago when I had no dishwasher or crock pot to set before leaving for work.

Now, my job-----just a job. Not a career. After all, my work must be scheduled around that of the children and husband. Why? As long as history has been recorded "it has been so."

Many times, I have fantasized about walking into an office bearing my name on a brass plate, wearing a dark business suit with matching shoes and jewelry with my hair professionally done in a smooth chignon. In reality, I have worked as waitress, stock clerk, file clerk, office girl Friday, nurse aide, sales clerk, whatever I could fit around husband and children. I was even licensed as a cosmetologist but found the hours did not fit around my family's needs. I gave other women fashionable hair styles and shiny shaped nails while I barely had time to dry my hair before leaving home. My hours were sometimes days, midnights, afternoons, many times weekends, anything necessary to earn an income and still fulfill my 'place', the jobs often boring, often tedious and usually, not really satisfying. Like most people, my childhood was filled with dreams of what I wanted to grow up to be and none of those jobs seemed to fit those dreams.

Children grow up and can be seen developing into responsible individuals. Husbands get promotions or change jobs for better positions. Is it any wonder I found myself Myra Enders, woman lacking something?

D.W.
DIVORCED WOMAN
D.W.
DELIGHTED WOMAN

At the age of fifty-three, I found myself a divorced woman although it took me almost two years to break completely free of those invisible bonds. It was definitely a shock to call myself a divorced woman due to my upbringing, but I soon realized I was also a delighted woman. The first few months were difficult because I found myself earning yet another set of letters—

W.L.O.S.S.
WOMAN LIVING ON A SHOE STRING

Living on a shoe string—a broken one at that. Years of the employment mentioned had not prepared me to be the sole support of a household which included a teenager. The almost two years of divorce proceedings were tedious for a number of reasons because as anyone who has ever been in that situation knows, there are still shared ownership issues and many financial things to be straightened out but after that long period of time, I finally had one more set of letters—free woman.

F.W.
FREE WOMAN

The word free took on a new meaning for me. The divorce truly set me free. Raised in a family of eight children and at age 19 becoming a full time stepmother and wife did not give me any time to have that freedom and independence most experience between fleeing their parent's nest and starting their own family. I simply went from being part of one household to being part of another with no time as a newlywed experiencing the new togetherness of just two people learning about one another. There was never that time to decorate just as I wanted to or eat just what and when I wanted. I hope my readers will not consider me selfish but for the first time in years, I was thinking of myself. And, I loved it.

I'm alive, I'm healthy.
I have time and space.
I have a few gray hairs
And wrinkles on my face.
I'm shorter. I'm thinner,
I have developed mature grace.
I can cook what I want.
I can cook when I wish.
I can finish a meal with only one dish.
I no longer heat hot dogs as I did in past years.
A week with no hot dogs meant kids with tears.
No more early morning pancakes

to fill hubby's plate.

I can get an early morning walk done

Before it gets late

I can actually read the news

And have tea while it's still hot.

I can properly dress for the day or relax a while and not.

I can do exercises while still in my gown or don a jogging suit and go downtown.

I can sit by the lake and watch the sun rise while streaks of color open the skies.

I can turn on the TV and watch my kind of show.

I can spin a CD and hear music I know.

The idea is, as you can see.

I live alone now,

This time's for me.

Living alone has truly made me a free woman.

C.D.
COLLEGE DEGREE

It had been my lifelong dream to have a college diploma and now, I have three, each prominently displayed in my home along with my gold honors cord and a picture of me walking to the stage in my blue robe and cap to pick up my diploma. It took me almost six years to earn that first one since I worked a full time job to earn my living and part time to pay for the classes. I had thought I could probably receive a grant but for the first time in my life, I was informed I made too much money. So, lots of hours of work and not enough sleep but I was determined to get that piece of paper in my hand. Never in my wildest dreams did I envision more than an associate degree but once started, I was hooked. Learning and reading have always been pleasurable for me and college allowed me to delve into topics I had previously only read about. For almost nine years I worked ungodly hours and spent more hours studying and doing research. I got through the first two degrees without having to struggle with math which has always been my waterloo. I managed that by substituting science or biology. It was an outstanding experience for a fifty something woman who graduated high school in 1954 to be going to classes with youthful students just out of high school. I probably would not have done well in the biology classes requiring lab except for group projects where I had much younger partners who had experienced lab classes in recent years. Never however, were any of those students disrespectful about my age. I had avoided math in any way I could but in order to obtain my general studies section requiring math, I could no longer avoid it. I admit to asking for the lowest level math I could use for the requirements. It still was daunting to me. From 1954 to 1999 much had changed. Modern math seemed like Greek to me. Fate was kind. During a class break, I met a girl just out of high school who was struggling with English and Literature. We were made for each other. Once a week, she came to my home and over pizza and Pepsi, with her younger brother watching TV across the room, we each tutored the other in the fields in which we were weak. One of the most important points I would like my readers to realize is that these young students *learned from me and I learned from them.* Never have I regretted the effort it took to be able to sign my name Myra Enders, G.R.N (gerontologist) or Myra Enders, LA (Liberal Arts) or Myra Enders, G.S (General Studies).

W.T.
WORLD TRAVELER

Throughout all the years of marriage, my husband and I drove through more than half of the states in our nation. He refused to fly so we truly 'saw the U. S. A. in our Chevrolet'. My foreign travel was limited to trips into Canada either through the tunnel or over the bridge. Both of these access venues were in Detroit, only about twenty-five miles from our home. Never did I think I would have a passport. Now, not only do I have one, I have used it several times. My first real trip to another country was a ten day excursion to London, England as an escort for a high school band in which one of my granddaughters participated. That band marched in the Queen's New Year's Day parade. The queen sat in an enclosed 'box' in a position that allowed participants and spectators to see her. I had so many great experiences while there. For example, I learned that if one orders hot tea, it automatically arrives at your table with milk in it. The server in a small 'tea house' I visited chuckled when he saw the expression on my face. He advised me that I needed to specify to the server that I wanted mine without milk. That little tea house probably did not seat more than 25 patrons at any one time and everyone seemed to know everyone else. I noticed that in London proper, there are many very small businesses. What I spoke of as London proper is often called 'the square mile' by residents because it is only 1.12 square miles in size, therefore, only a tiny part of the entire Metropolis of London. When I visited there, no super markets existed. My experience of shopping there was very interesting.

You must first realize that rain falls most every day, therefore, most carry umbrellas. One steps off a subway train with umbrella handle cupped over his arm, and stops at two, three, or perhaps four small shops on the way home. Here in America, we are accustomed to eating left overs but in London, most shop daily at these tiny shops. Each specializes in one type of food such as the 'green grocer' with his fresh fruits and vegetables, one for dairy, one for meats, one for fresh baked goods so one shopping for dinner will buy small amounts of food from several different places. Most daily subway riders live close enough to walk home. Most in that square mile live in apartments and most who live in that square mile do not own cars. The hectic traffic is comprised of cars traveling through the city to or from other places. And, hectic hardly describes the traffic well. It is fast, cars dangerously close to one another with intersections consisting of lines of cars from four or five directions all merging into one. There are so many cars that the streets are arranged with traffic lights just for pedestrians in the center of the streets. One can rarely walk all the way across a street without help from a red light. A truly amazing scene.

My first cruise visited only two Caribbean Islands—Freeport and Nassau. It was there I first experienced parasailing. What a beautiful sight to behold from a few hundred feet above the land and water. Even from that height, looking into the water was like looking into fine crystal. It was possible to see an entire underwater world. Those life specimens were more vividly colored than any I had ever seen. My second cruise visited four islands and my head was assailed with visual and auditory sensations. Two more cruises covered other areas and presented views of the world and people one cannot absorb just by reading a book. Having read about some of the places made my appreciation of them in person much more intense.

I have felt compelled to tell you of these adventures in my 'more mature' years, after my children no longer depended on me to make a specific point. I was not a woman of means, so months of work and saving went into being capable of paying for and taking time off work to enjoy them. For the most part, women of my age did things for children but not for themselves. Therefore, THIS TIME IS OURS. If we have given our children the best education we could and tried to pass along whatever wisdom we possessed, then we have done our duty and now, need to step back and allow them to make their own way as we made ours. Giving children everything does not give them the one thing necessary to make a successful person. That is the ambition to work and set a goal to work towards. They can work and save for these adventures and enjoy them all the more knowing it was their own initiative that made them possible. Do them a favor and allow them to know that pleasure. I can now truly say I am Myra Enders, world traveler.

C.E.
COMPUTER EXPERT

Well, to be perfectly honest, not exactly an expert. In fact, my children and grandchildren would laugh at that idea. I still need to call one of them sometimes (actually frequently) to ask why something isn't doing what I want it to do. Some days, I have thought about throwing it in the trash. It reminds me of that TV show called "Are you smarter than a 5th grader?" It is simply sharper than I am. And quicker. Just a touch of the wrong key and it is off and running to places unknown. After having a computer in my home for some over twenty years, changes still constantly make it necessary to learn something new. If making the brain work is truly a help in slowing the aging process, then this electronic contraption is a miracle because I can think of nothing else in my life that requires so much brain work. While still working, much of my time was spent working with seniors in a retirement village and the company sent me to Wayne State University in Detroit where I earned a certificate naming me a 'Senior Computer Mentor'. The idea was for me to teach senior residents how to use basic computer skills. So, I thought I was quite accomplished at the time. Now, 15 years from the time of my retirement, I am assembling this book on my fifth computer and should probably change my designation of Myra Enders, computer expert to Myra Enders, Computer Novice.

F.E.

FAMOUS ENTERTAINER

I suspect most anyone reading this epistle has at some time harbored the desire to be an entertainer---a singer or movie star. Our family was a musical one. Our mother had majored in Music and Bible and taught all of us music to whatever degree we would absorb it. We all had some degree of musical talent and mine was in singing. Of course, I had visions of being a famous singer, actress and dancer although I knew nothing about dancing. Our family quartet entertained frequently during my childhood and had a Sunday Morning Gospel Radio program during my school years. My piano playing talents definitely lacked star status. However, this did not dim my love for performing. After marrying and moving to another state, I soon found a woman with whom to sing duets in church. Years later when attending college, I needed credits in physical education and for those I chose modern dance and jazz. My instructor probably wondered what a mid-50s woman was doing in black leotards alongside young, agile girls just out of high school. Nevertheless, I earned top grades, probably more for persistence than ability. It was good exercise and led me to take a session of tap dance at a private studio. One of my granddaughters was taking dance lessons at a studio where an adult class was in danger of being cancelled due to lack of enrollment. One of my adult daughters, probably 40ish at the time, and I signed up just for fun. We completed the course, a few sore muscles, sore feet but no broken bones. At the end of the session, we participated in a dance recital wearing black harem outfits. What a challenge! What fun! The closing number that night consisted of dancers of all ages, each group in different costumes, and each group doing their dance and taking their place while other performed. It was a great learning experience for me. Those of you who recall the great musicals of years ago would have appreciated it. I tell this story in an effort to encourage you to take the plunge and do those things you have dreamed about. I recently read a quote by Tagore—"You can't cross a sea merely by standing and staring at the water." So, my advice to you is to step in, test the waters. You can always wade out if it gets too deep.

    I have an acquaintance in her 80s who has recently purchased a guitar. She took some piano lessons while still in school but never developed that skill very far. Years later, after retirement, after supporting herself and her son by working as a legal secretary, she took organ lessons and although she does not perform in public, she plays her beautiful organ for her own enjoyment. Although she never harbored an ambition of being a great actress, she did play several walk on parts with a local theatre group. So, why not a guitar now? Age really does not matter. I could give you several examples such as this. I once knew a man who, in his mid 40s, decided he wanted to learn piano and did. Like my 80 something year old friend, he learned it just for his own pleasure. No great talent is required. Just step forward and have fun. One does not have to jump in with both feet. First, just dip a toe in and test the waters. Then, try ankle deep, knee deep and if waist deep is too much, just wade back a bit and try again. Perhaps just that little trial will satisfy you. If so, fine. But, you will at least be able to say you tried. If you have made yourself or someone else laugh, you have been a successful entertainer. I have a ukulele, a guitar, a keyboard and an accordion. I do not play any of those instruments anywhere near professional, but I enjoy them. So, I have named myself Myra Enders, F.E.

W.P.
WRITER, PLAYWRIGHT

We have all had youthful dreams and ambitions being swept away by the reality of earning a living and taking care of family responsibilities. I count myself very fortunate to have been able to pick up some of those threads later in life.

My Red Hat group recently ventured to the Bayside Restaurant by the waters of Lake St.Clair, in New Baltimore, Michigan. I do not know which I enjoyed more, the crab stuffed flounder or the scenery; gulls sitting on pier posts, calling to other gulls, a light breeze and sometimes wind gusts fluttering the umbrella above out table. After lunch, we went to The Washington Street Wine House where we tasted several wines made in the area. Since they are located within a few yards of the lake, their décor is mostly nautical. It was there I saw the following quote: "If your ship hasn't come in, swim out and get it." I wish I had known that quote many years ago. Even though I just recently read it, I believe I have lived my live in that vein.

Writing has been a hobby of mine as long as I can recall. Happily, in my mid 50s, a great opportunity presented itself in the guise of a part time job when I was needing one to pay for college classes. A 150 unit retirement center needed an activity director. Their needs and mine coincided perfectly with mine.

Since they were not quite certain exactly what my duties would be, (This was the first in this company's chain of senior living centers to have an activity director) I was pretty well given free rein. My pay check had little to do with my enjoyment of that job. It was hardly like a real job. Although there were trips to plan, parties to be coordinated and educational events to be set up, the best of all for me was freedom to present performances, using senior residents and performing plays written by *me.*

Seniors who had never performed before now did so for numerous lunch time skits which I wrote about whatever important day it happened to be or about some historical person's birthday. For example, history records the fact that the marriage between George and Martha Washington was not a love match. Rather, it was more of a business deal. Martha, a widow, owned land but had no knowledge about how to manage it. George had the knowledge and experience but owned no land. A match made in heaven. It worked well except for George's roving eye. It did not however, rove very far. He only had one woman in his life other than Martha and he kept a relationship with her until his death. In our skit, Martha and the "other woman" came face to face. This was presented as a comedy with the characters dressed in appropriate costumes for the time and at the same time, it presented a bit of history.

One full length play that I wrote, *The Queen of Bingo,* was successful enough that we loaded actors, costumes and items for a set onto our bus and performed at a few other retirement centers.

One hilarious skit was a *Murder Mystery Lunch* during which residents were to solve the murder from clues in a 750 piece puzzle which was completed and displayed on a table in the center of the room. It had been on view for a few days before the actual event. As diners entered the room, they were met with a complete murder scene. Sprawled on the floor beneath the puzzle was a dead man (a dummy).

I wrote, directed and produced—you name it. I did it all. WOW! Talk about fulfilling a dream!

For one play, I needed a piano player and we had recently lost our volunteer pianist. With no budget to pay for one, I came up with the next best solution. Remember, in the early part of this story, I said no one would ever call me a pianist? I became one. Well, sort of. It's those pesky black notes—the sharps and flats—that give me the most trouble. My solution was to write words and music to the beginning and ending songs we needed using only white notes. It took me a few weeks to memorize the piano part, but it went off without a hitch. Another example of stepping out and doing what one enjoys without having any great talent for it. I doubt most people in the audience other than my close friends and family, knew I could play only a few other songs and not well at that. Hence, my additional letters of recognition as Myra Enders, W.P

S. J.
SPORTS JOCK

As a child, I was not much into sports of any kind. However, to be fair to myself, living in a farming family, there was not really much time for sports. We got plenty of exercise working. In those days, children could actually work. Too bad that is no longer true. Although I did not always enjoy it as a child, I realize it taught me a lot and left little time for getting into trouble. In those years, soft ball was the big sport but unfortunately, I could not hit the ball nor could I catch it. I was too afraid I would get hit. As a result, at school recess when teams were chosen, no one wanted me on their team. But I survived. One cannot be good at everything. However, at that age, it was difficult to accept.

Life proceeded and sports had no part in my life. Neither of my children cared about sports in school and I did not push them in that direction. I did once enroll my oldest daughter in tennis lessons but she had little interest. They did all take swimming lessons as I felt basic swimming skills necessary for anyone living in Michigan with lakes abounding as they do. I could not swim myself but did later learn enough to hold my own in a pool. The three girls took roller skating instructions, as that was a very popular activity during those years. I later learned from my youngest that I embarrassed her during her skating lessons by dressing her in a purple skating outfit. She said she was the only girl not wearing cutoffs or jeans.

Still, I never did anything in any 'sportsy' until I was a Camp Fire Girl leader for my second daughter.

When I was 5 months pregnant with my last daughter in 1972, the first March of Dimes Walkathon took place in our area. That sounded like a great project for the girls. They took pledges for the twenty mile walk but unfortunately, the morning of the walk turned out to be very cool and rainy. One by one, mothers of the girls called in to say their daughters could not walk in the rain. Determined to follow through, I took my two daughters, about 11 and 14, and we did the walk. Surprisingly, all three of us finished and were happy to be able to sit on the lawn of the court house where the walk had begun and ended and listen to the entertainment. A big mistake! Once I sat down, not accustomed to that much walking, my feet and ankles swelled so much I had difficulty getting into the car and driving home.

That got me started walking and I never stopped. I did every walkathons for every charity I saw promoted and ended up with a dresser drawer full of T shirts. Then, I tried a three mile run and finished it although I fast walked as much as I ran. I had coerced my youngest daughter to make that run with me but was never able to talk her into another. After a few years of 5 K and 10K runs, I worked myself up to a half marathon. All I will say is that I did finish it—all 13.1 miles.

These walks and runs took place over a few years and in between them, I did other things. Remember I wasn't wanted on my school soft ball teams. Well. I showed them! At about the age of 50, I joined a women's soft ball league. I was the oldest member of the team and we were not really very good. I still didn't catch or hit well even after my five year stint with the team, but by some fluke, we actually were one of the top teams in the league one year. I might add this was a church league so they could not very well refuse my participation.

I also did lots of bike riding in those years. The longest ride was for some charity and I rode seventy-five miles on my three speed bike. A short time later, one of my sons-in-law bought me a ten speed. Better late than never.

By pushing the envelope a bit, I can include two more activities as sports. Although I have been to Las Vegas several times, in 1995 and again in 1996, I went there with a dart league I had been participating in for about a year. We competed with leagues from several states and five countries. Shortly after my divorce, I was looking for some outlet that did not necessarily include couples. I happened across someone who was on a league and I participated for a couple of years before the opportunity for the 'Las Vegas" league had an opening I could fill. We were good enough to win enough to pay our expenses for the trip.

Another trip to Las Vegas was with a bowling league. I did not participate in the tournament in Vegas, rather just had fun by myself and took several tours. One day, when it was hot as …, I walked down one side of the strip and up the other, stopping in each casino. I collected a few tokens from each one to take home to my grandchildren. They were young enough at the time that they appreciated little things like that. Just a bit of trivia—the strip is not actually in the City of Las Vegas, rather in the county, just across the city border. I had lots of new experiences and lots of fun earning my letters, Myra Enders, S.J.

P.,W.
POET, WRITER

Lest my readers notice I used *writer* in an earlier section, this is a different kind of writing. In the first section, I spoke of writing plays and skits for performances. The writing I speak of now is poetry, articles, stories and books. This current text will be my first completed book but other pieces have been printed in various venues. One of my duties at my last place of employment, a 150 unit retirement center, was helping put a newsletter together. A regular feature was one page biographies of residents. It was not easy to tell a serior's life story in such a short space but I enjoyed the challenge and felt I was successful in doing so. As I interviewed those seniors for their biographies, I realized many of them had fantastic experiences and great stories to tell.

Another occasional feature was short stories written of course, by yours truly.

Poetry has always been a hobby of mine. In fact, I have, stored in my jewelry armoire, a hand written poem titled *My Nephews,* which I wrote when I was probably 14 years old. Even though it is written in pencil and the paper is browned and in danger of crumbling, it is still legible. That is how long I have been writing poetry.

Mostly, poetry has been written just for my own pleasure but a few years ago, I began submitting poetry to several publications. A well known writer's magazine paid me $25.00 for a poem. After that, eight of my poems were printed in a Michigan based magazine that unfortunately is no longer in circulation. I treasure those magazines which I have stacked in my book case and occasionally, I take them out and reread my work. I amassed more letters, Myra Enders, P.,W.

Most of my poetry is about real people or real places. The following two poems were written about my grandson, Johnathon, who is now eighteen years old.

My Grandson

Ten little fingers and ten little toes.

Two tiny ears and one tiny nose.

Wrinkled folds that cover two eyes.
Circles of color as blue as the skies.
Skin as soft as baby duck down
and antics that remind me of a tiny clown.
His head is covered with soft, fine hair.
His skin, though wrinkled, is ever so fair.
He wiggles and squirms all over the place.
Sometimes frowns, sometimes smiles on his little boy face.
Hands rolled into fists, both feet in motion.
Soft and smooth with the scent of lotion.
He is cuddly and happy most of the time.
And his little smile tells me he knows he is mine.

Obviously, this poem was written when he was a tiny baby. The following one was 11 years later.

Eleven Years Old
He's eleven years old now and growing fast.
The clothes and shoes his mother buys just don't seem to last.
The toes in his shoes are pushing the end.
His belt fits so tightly he can barely bend.
Buttonholes in his shirt front are starting to split.
The seat of his pants are almost too tight to sit.
So, it's down to the mall to buy outfits new.
Since he's growing so fast, he'll only get two.
Even his toys are growing. What he wants now costs more.
They no longer come from the Toys-R-Us Store.
Rather from Media Centers or electronic places.

New gadgets, new features with new names and faces.
Like an I-pod. What's that?
Or a PsP movie player that leaves the wallet flat.
These new 'toys' all so strange to me
need batteries or have to be powered by tv.
No more dirty rocks picked up from the ground.
Or odd shaped sticks found just laying around.
No more pockets filled with marbles or wings from a dead bee.
The things he wants now costs lots of moooooney.
Now, just a sign of the times this change may be
But it's not so simple as that it seems to me.
I've known him since he used a sippy cup.
I can see he's not just growing larger,
He's growing up.

S.S.
SUPER SPELLER

A few years ago, I entered a senior spelling bee. In my young school years, I was considered a good speller and represented my school in the county for three consecutive years. So, I thought, "I have got it made." Too quick to feel superior!! I was in the competition until the last day when only ten were present for the finals and a few strict rules. I was confident. Alas. Out of the ten, I was the third to sit down. So I didn't win. I met people. I laughed. I had fun and had a free lunch. Don't we all enjoy those? I was also inspired to purchase a new dictionary. Now, I realize young people today do not use dictionaries. They have computers, tablets and phones that can be used for word searches. I have those things also but I still enjoy holding a real paper book in my hands. This experience led me to declare myself Myra Enders, S.S.

A.A.
ACCOMPLISHED ARTIST

Accomplishments can run to any degree and I ask you not to judge to what degree I am accomplished. It was another of my dreams. Of course I did do some drawing as a child in school and with my children but other than that; my artistic ability with a brush had been completely sterile. After my children were grown and I had a bit of extra time, I decided to paint. Utter failure. So, not to be discouraged, I signed up for a few classes at a senior center and after a few months, realized I first needed some ability in drawing. A local community college offered classes in black and white drawing. Just what I needed and again, I suppose I mystified a teacher as to why I was there. However, I persevered and went on to another class for instructions in watercolor, oils, charcoal and pen and ink. OK. Art world here I come. No one saw any of my work for probably the first year but I realized I must be bold enough to show them sometime. My first public showing was for only three matching oils, no judging, just showing. I received a few compliments, enough to encourage me a bit. I donated one to a new senior housing site and they hung in it a hallway. At least, they didn't refuse it. Then, I got bold enough to enter a national contest just for artist over sixty-five and received an 'honorable mention' for it. I suspect every entrant was given an honorable mention but I was happy with mine. Those paintings were used to decorate the hallways in an international conference building in Washington, D.C. More bold than ever, I located a small gallery in Detroit, Michigan that displays only works by the over sixty-two crowd. I was astounded when I saw some of the great paintings created by hands older than mine. I was humbled. I was thrilled of course, when I was chosen "Artist of the Month" once and eleven of my paintings were placed on the walls of the small bistro in the rather well known senior affairs building across from Wayne State University. My one and only claim to fame as a real artist. Shortly after that, I was (through no fault of my own) involved in a serious accident which resulted in an injury to my brain stem and I learned something new. The brain stem helps control the movement of the eyes and that led me to have to give up further efforts towards painting. However, I had my season in the sun in the art world and was content. Hence, another designation—Myra Enders, A.A.

B.T.
BELOVED TEACHER

I adored my first teacher, Miss Minton, an old maid when it was not politically incorrect to use that term. She truly dedicated her life to teaching. My first school was a one room school for grades one through eight. No running water so no inside bathrooms. No electricity. No kindergarten in those days. At least not where my family lived, so at the age of just past five, I started first grade. According to rules, I should not have started until the next year but Miss Minton enrolled me early so she would have two students in the first grade. With one person teaching eight grades, she shifted students around so she did not have just one student in a class. It worked. One of my brothers completed three grades in two years and one of my sisters completely skipped the third grade. It worked well for her and for students also. Within my memory, there were no more than 30 students at any one time. When a student finished the eighth grade, he had to go to the "big" school which was still small enough that the entire school probably had no more than 150 students. . At the end of my fifth grade in 1946, with only 15 students remaining, my little country school was closed. As an adult I have realized we had an absolutely great education. Miss Minton was very strict and very demanding but fair. She expected us to do our best and settled for nothing less.

    We walked to school no matter what the weather conditions—at least a mile and a half morning and again in the afternoon. Had we walked all the way on roads, we would not have been there early enough so we cut across fields. I vividly recall being terrified of a blind mare that was in one pasture. She would follow our sounds and I was afraid she would step on me. We had to cross a creek at one point and since there was no bridge, we walked across on a large felled tree. On days when it had rained a lot, either our father of the father of some other kids who walked with us would come and meet us to make sure we got across safely. Snow or rain did not deter us.

    We were like the postman—neither rain, nor hail, not sleet, nor snow…….We had snow suits and rain coats and boots. In my first few years of school, our family did not own a car. We first got one when I was about ten years old.

In winter we were often cold and wet by the time we arrived at school and we would have our first class sitting around the coal burning stove so we could dry out and get warm. Sometimes, Miss Minton let us have hot cocoa and sometimes we made croquettes.

I know it is difficult to believe today, but we actually had 'inspection' each morning. She checked our hands and nails for cleanliness and asked about tooth brushing. On the back porch, each of us had a cup and tooth brush and a jar lid with a mixture of soda and salt. We brushed our teeth each day after lunch. I mentioned in the beginning of this section that we had no inside water. We pulled buckets of water from a well on the grounds.

Miss Minton taught us many things not printed in books and I credit her for a good start in my education. I wish today that I had found a way to let her to know while she was still alive how much I appreciated her.

Friday was activity day. She taught me to embroider and a bit of knitting and some simple stitching. One year, I made a luncheon cloth with matching napkins. I embroidered a pillow top with a picture of a kitten in an airplane. We did glass painting. One year, we built a bird sanctuary in the wooded area next to the building and each of us made a bird house or bird feeder. No purchased kits from the store to just put together. We drew patterns on wood, used a coping saw to cut the pieces, painted the pieces and then nailed them together. I believe I was the youngest that year and I made a feeder using just four pieces of wood.. Now, since we had built that sanctuary and kept food out, Miss Minton explained that we may have discouraged some of the migrating birds from leaving so it was our responsibility to make water and food available for them through the winter.

Another year, we grew a garden with each student being responsible for one vegetable. Since this was a farming community, we all had large gardens at home but she insisted we do this on our own.

Every morning, we sang a couple patriotic songs and did exercises—after walking that distance. We had exercise rods made from broom handles, painted red, white and blue. This was a patriotic period in our lives. One year, we filled boxes to send to service men with items such as tooth brushes, combs, stamps, post cards, writing tablets and other small items. I am confident every student in the school had at least one relative away from home due to our involvement in World War II. My siblings and I had three uncles in different branches of the service and in different locations in the world. One was at Pearl Harbor when it was bombed and two others in Germany so it is easy to understand why patriotism was so strong.

We performed plays sometimes and always had shows for each holiday.

When that school closed and I had to go to the larger school, my first teacher there—sixth grade—was also an 'old maid'. I loved her as much as I did Miss Minton. Is it any wonder I had ambitions of being a teacher? Since I had not been to college after high school graduation, I had no teaching qualifications. But, the yen for teaching stayed in my mind. Over the years though, I did do some teaching. Of course, I taught my own children and grandchildren and tutored three foreign students who had immigrated to the U.S. just a few weeks before time for school to start that fall. They were in middle school at that time and I worked with them until their first year of college when they had surpassed me in everything other than English and Literature.

Later, after I did have my college degrees, I taught Michigan History, drawing and creative writing at a home school co-op and worked one school year with a third grade class at a "Blue Ribbon" school. I felt I had earned my letters for Myra Enders, B.T.

E.G.

ELECTRONIC GURU

Yes, me, seventy-eight years old and continually learning new 'stuff' every week, perhaps every day. As to why it is important for me to tell you, my readers, about this, you must understand my background in this field. As a child, my family did not have a telephone. Most people today cannot fathom living without one but we survived quite well. Progress, however, has a way of evading every corner of the world and our corner could not escape that intrusion.

I was about seven years old when we had our first telephone installed. It was a wooden box fastened to a wall and calls were made by using a hand crank. An 'operator' would make the calls for us other than just close neighbors.

We were on a party line which means that although only one conversation could be taking place at any one time, anyone on that line could listen in and I think that was a favorite past time of a few. Of course, it seemed almost like a miracle to us. Still, we did not use it a lot because being on a farm which required outside work off and on all day; we were limited as to the hours of a day that we could even hear it ringing.

In 1956, when I married and moved into a city, I had a black rotary phone which set on a table. I say we had a black phone because in those years, all of them were black. They were provided and maintained by Michigan Bell, the only telephone company available and only later could one purchase phones in different colors. A few years later, princess phones became available and they had cords long enough that the user could walk a few feet from the connection and still talk. We still had party lines with multiple families on the same line. If I recall, in 1956, my Michigan Bell telephone bill was $6.00 a month.

Then some brilliant politician decided it was unfair to us to not have more than one company to choose from and declared Michigan Bell a monopoly. So, we now have the privilege of choosing from many different phone companies, pay an enormous price for the actual phone as well as for its use. In fact, our government feels so strongly that we should all have a cell phone, they are now offered *free* to people in certain income levels.

I enjoy caller ID and voice mail but could easily live without either. I could live without a camera or video or recorded music on my hand held devices which for most people I know has become almost like an appendage to their hands.

Years rolled by and a mobile phone was invented which was large, bulk, heavy and was powered by batteries.

Then, cordless phones came along and we thought nothing more could be dreamed up. They sat in bases that kept them electrically charged and some could be used in different rooms or even outside if not too far away from the base. Then cell phones small enough to fit into one's hand. They mostly just made and received calls. Now, I have a 'smart' phone which is smarter than most humans I know and does amazing things. It takes pictures, even videos with sound and has the capability of taking pictures and forwarding them to other cell phones of even transferring them to computers. One can download a program that enables her to read books on her cell phone. They have dictionaries, encyclopedias, games and other capabilities too numerous to enumerate.

While these things were transpiring, computers came along. I have read that our government had a computer system during World War II but certainly not anything like the ones we use today. The public did not have computers until years later. We did have microfiche, a system of storing large amounts of data on microfilm. I once worked in an office where we used those machines and we thought it was the epitome of modern technology. Alas, still more was to come.

I first touched a computer in about 1988 and never dreamed I would actually own one. As well as I can remember, I became the proud owner of one about 22 years ago. It was much larger than those in use today. Between the monitor and speaker, it took up the entire top of my desk. I have learned a lot since then and just about the time I think I have something down pat, things change. Someone always thinks they can build a better mouse trap. Keeping up with just the basics of computer use certainly keeps one on her toes.

Why have I called myself a technology guru? I now have not only the computer I am using to write this book. I also have a tablet which will do just about everything my computer will do and of course, a modern cell phone that does amazing things. Can you imagine reading a book on my computer or on my tablet or on my cell phone? I can pick up any of those devices and find the next page 'book marked'. I can download eBooks from my local library on either of those devices without charge and have reading materials with me anywhere I go without having to handle a bulky book although I do still thoroughly enjoy holding a book in my hands. I can send typed messages on the tablet or cell phone. The phone does numerous other things that I do not even know how to explain. I have a Face Book account, a Twitter account and email addresses with two different servers. Hence one more lettered designation—Myra Enders, E.G.

P.V.
PROFESSIONAL VOLUNTEER

I speak of being a professional volunteer not so much because of *what* I have done, rather the huge amount of time invested. Like most mothers, I was heavily involved in any and all activities at my children's schools. Our girls were Girl Scouts in their elementary years but when we moved to a more rural setting, we found no Girl Scout troops available so I started a Camp Fire Group. Earning merit badges for that organization involved doing for others so I found some volunteer projects worked well. This led me to some volunteer services for myself. My first serious project was working at blood banks with the Red Cross. It was a convenient involvement because I could take my eleven year old daughter with me. Eleven year olds could be given assignments there as long as a parent was present so at that age, my youngest got involved in the life of volunteering and I feel this has had an impact on her life. She later served as a Candy Striper at a hospital and after serving over 600 hours, received recognition from our State Representative. My oldest daughter worked with a county project serving physically and mentally impaired young adults.

My involvement with the Red Cross ended after about five years when another position caught my attention. I initially attended a six week program about visitation in hospitals and that led me to another program at another hospital where I served for some over five years as a Pastoral Associate. That involved being on call when a death occurred or was imminent and I would talk to family members about organ donation and tissue transplants. A rewarding experience.

Stored away in my file cabinet are certificates showing I logged over three hundred hours as a volunteer for the Michigan State Fair. Now before you say something like "WOW", I point out that I was one of over 500 seniors who did the same thing. I have lived in Michigan just under 60 years and never questioned how our great state fair was financed. I just assumed it was a money making machine since everything seemed to cost a lot. It came as a surprise to me to learn that the state had been subsidizing it and our governor, after many years, decreed that the fair had five years to become self-supporting and then, the state would cease to support it.

The call for help went out to all of the senior sites in the area and over 500 of us felt the fair was too much of a tradition to lose. For two years, we donated time, sweat and muscle in return for a free T shirts and free lunches. Hey! Seniors always love a free lunch. They let me do several different things and it was exciting to me to be involved in the workings of such an event. Great fun and great experiences.

About eight years ago, I learned of a program for seniors over the age of fifty-five. Catholic Charities of South Eastern Michigan places volunteers in school settings to serve with 'at risk' children. The Foster Grandparent Program has been in force for 50 years and gives emotional and educational support to children in need of just a bit of that extra something. Sometimes, just a touch of love or understanding. Working with young children in need is both challenging and uplifting. The seniors make a difference in the lives of the children and the children make a difference in the lives of the seniors. Although I am familiar only with the program in Michigan, it is a national program and has volunteers in several states. Most schools welcome any help offered and most children respond to a helping hand.

My second daughter is president of an organization called MI-HOPE Michigan, with a goal of providing drug awareness and education. If you would like information, check out their web site at mi-hope.org. Recently, I spent a day with her at a fund raising golf outing at the Pontiac Country Club for this organization and we raised some over $7,900.00. Several volunteers worked tirelessly for hours, much of it outside in the sun, but all enjoyed being part of a successful event for a worthwhile cause and we had great company and great fun as well as, you guessed it...a free lunch provided by the country club. The Pontiac Country Club was very helpful and cooperative. Have you noticed how many events I attend where there is a free lunch?

Each year, our local senior center hosts a fund raiser for Meals On Wheels and up until two years ago, I did the walk for which pledges are taken. Then, I decided it was time for me to start doing something inside the building that required a bit less effort. Another free lunch for those who gave of our time and effort. There is always something that needs doing.

The Light House, an organization known for providing emergency help hosts a 'Walk For Hunger' each year and I did that for twelve years.

These are things that the average person can do and most of them cost the participant nothing other than time and effort.

Jump on the band wagon! Numerous organizations need help. If, like me, you have more time than money, why not give some of that time to some worth while cause? Money is needed of course, but in some cases, your time is just as important.

One word of caution. If the organization asking for help is one you are not familiar with, check into it and make certain it is above board and supports something you are passionate about. Then, GO TO IT!

As you can see, by volunteering myself, I have encouraged my children to do the same. I believe all three of my daughters would say, if asked, that volunteering is rewarding.

V*alid cause.*

O*ne helper can sometimes seem like an army.*

L*ove for your fellow man is enough reason.*

U*nending need is always in your vision,*

N*ever doubt that you might someday need help.*

T*op spirits will be your reward.*

E*veryone has something to give.*

E*nough? There's never enough that more will not be appreciated.*

R*emember, helping one is helping all.*

PART II

I feel fortunate to be part of a family of readers. One of my earliest memories of our father is of him reading the newspaper from front to cover after supper and after a day of hard labor on our farm. Mother didn't read so much but as I look back, I realize it was for lack of time. She cooked, sewed, cleaned and did laundry for ten people. For a few years, she wrote a neighborhood column for our local paper.

I am speaking of days before children had video games, computers and cell phones to play with. We had more time to read and were encouraged to do so. At one time, I had read all the books in my high school library except for the research section of course, so one of my teachers would go to another school and bring books for me.

Eight years ago, I began keeping a list pf books I have read and I have now recorded 816. I quickly point out those were not little paper back romances-----rather *real* books. I have read some in years past when I was working many hours and could only read a chapter at a time between shifts. I suppose my favorite genre is mysteries but I also read non fiction, biographies and autobiographies. I have three sisters and one brother still living and all are readers. One sister and the one brother probably read more than I do.

Most of my close friends are avid readers and some feel short stories are passe. However, out local library has an entire section of short story collections. I enjoy reading and writing them

so..., here
goes...…....

BITTER BUTTER

Maggie buried the plunger one last time into the lid of her grandmother's wooden churn. Wiping perspiration from her face with her every day apron, she rested the weight of her ample body on the plunger. The rounded end, worn smooth by three generations of use, pushed painfully into her chest. Ignoring it, she struggled to catch her breath. Despite the discomfort, she struggled to finish churning this butter. She was determined to have fresh butter to serve the quilting ladies.

"What a day to be churning butter", her husband said earlier as he left for a short drive to Al's Market, the only store for miles without going all the way to town. Al's stocked most things needed in a farming community: flour in 25 pound bags, sugar and corn meal beside stacks of denim overalls, straw hats, boots, canning jars, a few pots and pans, horse liniment shelved next to Vicks and Bengay, bolts of fabric along with sewing necessities.

A small glass case held wheels of cheese and ten pound sticks of bologna waiting to be sliced into smaller chunks for customers. Some days, a container of homemade butter set beside the bologna. Miz Thomas brought over what she didn't use, but not to sell. Al had instructions to give it to anyone who wanted it.

Miz Thomas lived alone now that her husband had passed on and her children exchanged farm dust and crop uncertainty for bright lights and city traffic. Her arthritis made it difficult for her to reach up to her head-height rows of nests for laying hens, so she had stopped raising chickens. She could get eggs at Al's left there by neighbors just as she left her excess butter. His store served as a sort of trading place for neighbors.

A few straight backed chairs, upturned apple crates and a couple empty barrels clustered around the wood-burning stove. In cold weather, work shoes shod feet protruding from overalls rested on stacks of stove wood. The aroma of coffee filled the air. No sign proclaimed a charge for coffee, but nickels, dimes and quarters dropped into a green Mason jar always covered its cost. Al wasn't concerned about profits from the coffee; it helped keep the men lingering long enough to work up an appetite for bologna sandwiches, quite a profitable enterprise some days.

July 28, 1932 however, was not a hot coffee day. Orance Crush, Nehi Grape and RC Cola were the favored drinks when temperatures brushed 90° in Alabama's cotton country.

"How do Ben?" greeted Al. "How's the missus farin' in this heat?"

"Well, you know Maggie and her butter. Quiltin' bee's today and she wouldn't dream of not having fresh butter for the women folk. Never can understand why they want hot bread on such a hot day."

Ben plucked an RC from the cooler and flipped a nickel on the counter. His fellow farmers teased him. "Too hot for man or beast to be workin' fields but you left the little woman home alone slavin' over a churn?"

The men talked about how long the heat wave might last, how long before creek beds started drying up and ponds taxed to satisfy thirsty stock. They decided to help Dick Mitchell finish his new barn. Their wives would be at Maggie's home sharing news and gossip while quilting a 'Texas Star'.

The men had been working only a short time when screeching brakes and screams announced two of the wives. They ran toward the men, both frantically talking at the same time.

"She's dead! D.E.A.D. On the kitchen floor beside that old churn. Betty called the sheriff. Oh! It's awful."

Ben raced home in his dusty old Ford pickup, sliding to a stop behind the sheriff's car.

The scene that met him was shocking. Maggie lay in a circle of butter softened to an almost liquid state by the sweltering heat. The overturned churn had rolled beneath the kitchen table. Ben reached out and pulled the long gathered skirt of her dress down to cover her legs. He saw her cotton stockings which were worn by most country women, rolled neatly down to just about her ankles. He often wondered why bother wearing them in summer since the long dresses covered her legs anyway. However, Maggie was nothing if not proper.

A hundred thoughts raced through his mind. *How? Why? Did she accidentally turn the churn over and slip in spilled cream?* Ben was certain butter had been formed before the spill. Butter formed and separated from the remaining whey was the only explanation for the cloudy liquid he saw pooled under the stove. He knew her habits well. She never removed the lid until she was ready to remove the finished butter. Instead, she raised the plunger just enough to get a sample to spread on a slice of bread. She was a stickler for perfection when it came to her butter. On the floor near her outstretched hand lay a biscuit left over from breakfast, generously spread with butter, partially eaten; now resting against a chair leg. Crumbs were scattered on the floor as if it had hit with some force as it was dropped.

The sheriff, who crouched down in the kitchen, served the entire county and knew all of its residents on a first name basis. Many a time, Maggie had traded him a dish of butter for a pint of his wife's blackberry jam. Sheriff Henry said he could call for help. Nothing like this had ever happened during his years of being in office.

He didn't tell Ben he saw things that made him wonder about it being an accident. He noticed a brindle cat over in one corner hadn't moved a muscle even with all the activity in the room. *What cat would sleep through half a dozen women in a panic? What cat wouldn't be happily lapping up some of the butter?* The cat was dead---just like Maggie.

About thirty minutes passed before the sheriff from the next county arrived with an ambulance close behind. Sheriff Henry went outside to speak privately with the new arrival, officer Billings. He related what he had observed. Then the two officers walked back inside with the ambulance attendant.

The attendant checked for a pulse and as was already certain, found none. He estimated she had been deceased for possibly two hours. Ben blanched at that information. That means she died very soon after he left home to enjoy visiting with his friends. While he drank RC Cola and laughed with them, Maggie died. He knew he would always feel guilty.

The two officers helped the attendant take Maggie's body to the ambulance and along with Ben, followed it to the nearest hospital which was almost forty miles away. Ben didn't understand. *Why not just take her to the funeral home in town?* He didn't realize the officers had already decided this was a case of murder. He had not seen them bag the cat and take him along as well.

When Ben pulled the front door closed and started to his car, Sheriff Henry told him to go back and lock both front and back door. The sheriff intended having more qualified officers out to check things more thoroughly. They would have more equipment than he did. He had taken pictures but there was much more that needed to be done.

Ben resisted having an autopsy performed but he was convinced it was the only way to discover how Maggie died. He stayed overnight with a sister who lived nearby but didn't sleep well so he drove home before daylight and was surprised to find his house ablaze with lights and several men preset. Sheriff Henry was clearly agitated. He asked Ben how the kitchen came to be spotless and in perfect order. Ben denied any knowledge of it and the sheriff believed him.

Ben explained that most people around didn't even lock their doors and most who did used only old skeleton keys, which could probably open most doors in the neighborhood. The sheriff quickly dispatched officers to speak with neighbors in an effort to learn who had disturbed the murder scene.

Little time was needed as Bertha Dickens who lived about a mile away explained she cleaned up because she felt it was the least she could for a friend. She even scrubbed the churn with a brush, advising them that the brush was on the back porch shelf because it was still wet when she left. She was just being neighborly, she said.

As the officers gathered back at Ben's property, a clean picture was emerging. No everyone shared Maggie's opinion of her butter. A few had become resentful of the talk of her butter at all community events and at least a couple felt Maggie took just a bit too much pride in her claim to fame. After all, every farm wife for miles around did the same thing Maggie did—use fresh cream. And, every woman knows using fresh cream is risky. Depending on what cows had been grazing on, the cream could be sweet, or occasionally, a bit bitter. "Well, I for one just didn't think her butter tasted any better than anyone else's." This was the sheriff's first clue. *Did other women share Bertha's feelings?*

Two days later, the autopsy revealed that Maggie and the cat had been poisoned with lye. Tests showed the butter contained the highly toxic substance. All of the women used lye to make soap but they knew how to be careful with it. It caused acid burns to the skin unless used in highly diluted form and was known to cause chemical burns if taken by mouth and blindness if it got in the eyes. It was an agonizing thought to imagine Maggie dying in this way. When Al heard the cause of death, he immediately called Sheriff Henry and told him that Maggie had taken Miz Thomas's butter for the last few weeks. Al thought Miz Thomas might also be in danger if the butter was what killed Maggie.

Sheriff Henry and Ben immediately drove to the Thomas farm. Miz Thomas was indignant about being questioned but also seemed happy to have a chance to vent her anger at Maggie. "I always wondered why Maggie took my butter", Miz Thomas said. "She always boasted about her own." Miz Thomas said she had recently taken some cornbread and greens to Mr. Bolten, an elderly widower a few farms over, and when she saw one of her own dishes on his table, he told her Maggie had been bringing him a dish of butter almost every week for some time. "Now I ask you young man, if I was poisoning the butter I left at the store, how would I have known Maggie would take it? And how would I have known she would pass it along to Mr. Bolten without telling him it was mine? And, if it was my butter that killed Maggie, then kindly explain why *he* isn't dead." Gnarled hands, stiff and swollen with arthritis, wiped tears of anger and hurt from her eyes. Without waiting for an answer, she turned and sat wearily down in her porch swing.

    Ben, standing beside Sheriff Henry was stunned. It was true Maggie had passed the butter along to old man Bolten. She never used it herself. She thought she was doing two good deeds in one action: letting Miz Thomas feel needed and giving an old man a touch of joy in his lonely world. Murdered for doing a favor for old friends.

    Sheriff Henry decided he needed to talk to Bertha again and ask if she had seen anything unusual when she cleaned up the murder scene. As they neared the Dickens farm, they saw smoke rising from somewhere behind the barn. Thinking it might be a wild fire spreading due to recent heat and little rain, they ran toward the source of smoke and were surprised to see Bertha throwing dry leaves on an already blazing pile of brush. She was startled when she saw them and became almost irate when they attempted to douse the fire with buckets of water from the pond. Sheriff Henry was telling her how dangerous it was for her to burn brush with no one around to help in case it spread when Ben yelled, "That's Maggie's churn." As he had been trying to rake away some of the brush not yet blazing, he had uncovered a wooden churn.

Bertha crumbled into a heap on the ground, sobbing, talking incoherently, and babbling. "I didn't mean for her to die. I just wanted her to get sick, as sick as I was of hearing about her sweet butter." The story erupted from a very angry Bertha; a woman Maggie had considered a good neighbor and friend. Everyone knew Maggie stored her old churn on the enclosed back porch and also that she made fresh butter for every quilting bee. Maggie had a large dining room where she had set up a quilting frame and since there were no children in the house, she was able to leave it there from week to week. For that reason, the quilting bees were usually held in her house and according to Bertha, gave her an opportunity to fish for compliments on her butter. She said Maggie always served fresh yeast bread or muffins or scones or something that needed butter spread on it.

During the last meeting, while the neighboring farm women were working on a Texas Star quilt for a soon to be married couple, Bertha felt she had had her fill of Maggie's butter. While everyone was talking, Bertha left the group to visit the toilet, which was located near the shelf where Maggie stored her lye soap and bleach for laundry. An idea struck her. Picking up a bar of the soap, she quickly lifted the lid from Maggie's churn, another thing that was a sore spot for bertha's pride, and rubbed it over the bottom and side of the churn. She even rubbed it on the bottom of the churn's lid and over the sides of the plunger. "Not too much", she thought. Maggie was such a stickler for cleaning that she would notice any powder so Bertha dipped a dish towel in water , wrapped it around a chunk of soap and rubbed it vigorously over the inside of the churn, hoping she had caused any residue from the dry soap to blend into the old wood. After washing her hands, she returned to the dining room and realized the women had been so intent with quilting and talking, they hadn't seemed to even notice her leaving or returning. She took her place and tried to pick up the thread of conversation about how the heat was ripening the tomato crop before they had time to mature properly.

"Oh. I am sorry. I didn't mean for her to die. I just wanted to teach her a lesson. I dragged my own churn over to her house when I went to clean the kitchen and brought hers back here. My. What a job. Right through the corn field. I never realized a churn could be so heavy. I guess I am just a useless, jealous old woman. I was even jealous of her old churn. She claimed it came to America on the Mayflower! Maybe it did. But, who cares now? It is burned enough it can never again be used." Bertha stood, still frantically crying. "Just let me go inside and get my purse."

Several minutes passed and Bertha did not return. Sheriff Henry motioned to Ben to go around to the back door while he entered the front, thinking possibly she was trying to leave. As he opened the door, he heard the sound of breaking glass, followed by a thud. He rushed toward the kitchen and saw Bertha writhing on the floor, holding her throat, choking, eyes wide with fear, shock, and pain.

On the floor was a broken glass and splashes of water. A container labeled 'lye' set on the table, its lid nearby. A spoon, apparently used to stir a deadly combination of water and lye, was still clutched in one hand.

Sheriff Henry realized there was nothing he could do. She would be dead before medical help could arrive. Ben turned away, unable to look at her, realizing his Maggie had suffered the same way.

Now, the people of Cottonwood County would be attending two funerals in one week.

NO MINT FOR THE BOSS

A plain-clothes policeman who gave the appearance of having eaten too many doughnuts stood with his hands in the pockets of his rain-drenched trench coat studying the scene before him. The faint scent of mint teased his nostrils as he looked, without touching, at the items on an expensive looking glass-topped desk. The heavy glass protruded slightly off one end. A sliver of lemon soaked a white linen napkin. On one corner of the desk set a full cup of tea. Nearer the center of the desk set a delicately patterned teapot. The matching cup lay in a circle of wet carpet at the base of a nearby filing cabinet and the saucer had fallen into the waste basket. Two people sharing a morning cup of tea? Officer Blake checked his notes. Maureen Streeter, CEO of MIG International.

Miss Frank, Maureen's secretary, stood shaking outside the office door, using already damp tissues in an effort to stem the flow of tears. She had called 9-1-1 after finding the company president draped over the arm rest of her chair. An ambulance had taken the unconscious Maureen away and Miss Frank was left to meet the police.

"I don't understand officer," the secretary said. "Miss Streeter never drinks mint tea. She considers herself a connoisseur of teas, but detests mint."

"Yes", Officer Blake said almost to himself. "Here we see two cups and a teapot with the distinct scent of mint still present. Who would she have had in her office this early?"

"No one" said Miss Frank. "I normally am the first to arrive and have the day's appointments schedule waiting on her desk. However, I had arranged to come in an hour later today. I cannot imagine any other staff sitting down with her in the morning. She maintains her privacy and normally, no one other than me enters her office uninvited."

"A stickler for rules, huh?"

'Oh yes. And mint tea? I can't imagine it. I know she has a number of food allergies and I think she is probably allergic to mint. She often purchases packages of assorted teas and passes the mint on to Richard Dawson, her assistant whose office is next door."

"Miss Frank, I noticed two umbrellas set down to dry in the outer office", said Blake. "I assumed they belonged to you and Miss Streeter. But what about the person sharing that tea earlier?" I ran through a downpour after I parked my car."

'Oh, I don't know. I took a cab as usual and the driver pulled right up to the curb so I just made a mad dash. I cannot think who the second belongs to."

Officer Blake asked Miss Frank to show him the assistant's office. She led him a few steps down the hallway leading from the reception area and found Dawson's office locked.

"That's strange", said Miss Frank, puzzled. "I have never known this door to be locked. Miss Streeter insists on having availability to all of the offices at all times. Of course, I probably have a key to the door in my desk but have never used it."

"Your boss sounds very severe, insisting on access to offices yet not allowing staff to enter her office without invitation."

"Well, yes. You could say that. It's just that she works really hard and doesn't like interferences. It is a family business, you know. Her grandfather started his business in a two room second story office at a time when people were still suffering from the tragedies of the depression. His family thought it a foolish venture and refused to help, sure it would be a failure. He was just as determined to succeed and succeed he did. This is the third generation and MIG has steadily grown until it is now an international business. Many have tried to buy her out but Maureen has not relinquished control and in fact, she personally oversees every department."

"That must keep her busy."

"Well, she has hand- picked managers in each department and actually, promoting Mr. Dawson to her assistant was her first concession towards giving up any control. Richard is the perfect example of a man who worked his way up from the bottom. He started in the mail room a few days before I was hired as a junior typist in the secretary pool and both of us have risen in position and salary throughout our fifteen years with the company. When Miss Streeter became CEO, she personally chose me as her personal secretary. Still, she expects diligence."

Miss Frank triumphantly held up a set of keys and handed them to Officer Blake.

"Let's see why this door is locked."

The opened door revealed a rather ordinary office. A well -worn chair set behind a serviceable desk with papers strewn across it in disarray.

"Oh my," whispered the secretary. "If Miss Streeter saw this desk, she would not be happy at all. She keeps order in her office and expects it in other's as well."

The officer walked around the room, observing every detail; an unwashed mug in the miniscule sink in a corner kitchenette, damp tea bags in the waste basket and a white powdery substance sprinkled across the corner of the desk and some on the carpet. The other item that caught his eye led him to believe Dawson had already been in the office and left.

"Miss Frank, what time does Dawson usually come in?"

"That's another strange thing." She turned around as if inspecting the room herself. "He normally would have been here already. Miss Streeter expects punctuality."

As the two entered Miss Streeter's office again, Dawson, folding an umbrella as he walked, hesitated when he saw them.

"Oh Richard!" Miss Frank began. "You're late. Miss Streeter would......"

"Mr. Dawson. And I do not punch a time clock. Does Maureen know you are entertaining in the office?"

"Maureen? Mr. Dawson?" The secretary floundered for words. "Miss Streeter......."

'MR. DAWSON." I am Officer Blake with the Waterford Police Department and I need a few words with you."

"What's going on?"

After Dawson was informed that his unconscious boss had been taken away by ambulance, he appeared distraught. "If only I had been here. Maybe I could have done something."

"You were here," Blake said. "And, it appears you did do something."

"What are you saying?" Dawson said this as he walked to his office. He turned when he found his door unlocked and said, "Just what's going on here?"

"Cut the act, Dawson. Your other umbrella was drying in the lobby when I got here earlier. Your trench coat is drying on the coat rack and you left soggy tea bags in the waste basket. You have a white smudge on your tie which I am willing to bet will match the powder you left on your desk and sprinkled on your carpet. But my bets don't count. Our lab can verify that."

Dawson grabbed his brief case and started to flee but encountered another officer blocking his path. Officer Blake stepped closer, hands on his hips, coat opened to give a full view of his revolver. "What happened this morning? Did you make a pass and she turned you down? She is a beautiful woman."

Dawson glanced at the door once again, then sat down in the nearest chair, head in hands and shuddered. "It wasn't fair." Between clenched teeth he went on. "She was such a witch!"

"Was?" The detective allowed Dawson enough rope to hang himself.

"She deserved to die. She's been killing me slowly for years. Why couldn't she make me a partner? I was working here while she was still in college."

Words of venom spewed from Dawson's mouth. "She got a new desk. I got her old one. Same with the computer. She got a new eighteen inch screen monitor. I got her old out dated one. Even the damned tea! She didn't like mint so she generously *gave* it to me." He paused, looked around the office. "I came in early this morning and she told me, *told me* to make her a pot or tea. I made her mint and she yelled at me to make her *Lady Gray*. I left the cup of mint setting there. Who did she think she was? I was not her slave, but I did make her another pot of tea, a very special tea. I had had enough of her ordering me around. Why couldn't she treat me like an equal?"

"You'll be able to ask her yourself. She's alive, no thanks to you."

"Alive? I tho..thought….."

As Dawson was being taken away in handcuffs, the senior detective answered a call on his cell phone.

"Good thing he confessed. The lady he called a witch just died. Don't think I'll ever take another sip of tea."

MAGNETIC MURDER

A sign on the door read "No smoking. Oxygen in use" in large letters. The chart above his hospital bed informed one and all that the bed's occupant was Robert Duffy, date of admission 8-11- 2014. NPO (nothing by mouth).

In fact, tubes taped in place left no space for anything else in his mouth. More tubes trailed from IV trees on either side of the partially elevated metal frame. Drops of liquid slowly dripped through several feet of clear soft plastic.

Limp hands rested, palms upward, where they had been placed on top of the pristine white sheet covering the rest of his body, up to his chest. Eyelids flicked, eyes shifted slightly in vague recognition as steady hands slipped a copper colored bracelet around his right arm, just above his wrist.

The slim white uniformed figure slipped noiselessly from the room and down the hallway, past nurses settled in for the night with feet propped up and fresh mugs of tea at hand. With change of shift, rounds finished, problem sleepers sedated and lights dimmed, the next few hours would be spent catching up on paper work. Unless a patient pushed the call button, there was no need to enter patient's rooms for the next few hours.

The white uniform barely caught the security guard's attention as its wearer exited the Intensive Care Unit. Its wearer went home and sank blissfully into a recliner with a pot of piping hot Constant Comment tea and a paper back novel. Robert Duffy should be resting peacefully and hopefully, permanently.

The tea emitted an enticing aroma, just a hint of orange peel and spices. She was savoring the luxury of sipping from a delicately patterned, paper-thin china cup, part of an antique tea service which, because of its value, was normally displayed in a locked glass enclosed cabinet. Tonight however, circumstances were anything but normal.

She pushed the red power button on a multi-function remote and the fifty-six inch flat screen television came to life. *Law and Order* would start in ten minutes.

The ending of an *NYPD* rerun would keep her occupied until then. The paper back on her lap was for reading during commercials.

This would no doubt be a sleepless night for her. After all, she didn't want to appear at the hospital in the morning looking too fresh and well rested. Perhaps dozing in a recliner and staring at a flashing screen would give her that hoped for haggard look.

A check on *TV Guide* assured her of an enjoyable if not restful night. A six-hour marathon of *Law and Order* would keep her alert for a few hours. Then, *LA Law, The Practice* and *Matlock* would lead into the early morning news. Thanks to the new TV dish, detective shows were available at most any hour, but so much violence was not her style. She preferred more subtle means of murder.

At the hospital, the silence in ICU was broken by beeping machines. Nurses rushed to the source—Robert Duffy's room. His heart rate was erratic, faint and registered only 40 on the monitor. A quick check showed all of his tubes properly in place. There seemed to be no rational reason for this sudden change. "Drats" thought nurse Richards as she spied the bracelet on the patient's arm. Mrs. Duffy had been told that no jewelry was allowed on ICU patients. She was certain it had not been there when Mrs. Duffy left for the night. As nurse Richards removed it, she thought she would need to warn all other personnel to watch that Mrs. Duffy didn't put it back on. Perhaps she would just keep it at the nurse's station. The nurse thought perhaps it had some special meaning since Mrs. Duffy seem determined to have her husband wear it. But, rules are rules. Aside from the basic rules, this copper colored bracelet interfered with the tubing snaking from and around IV punctured arms.

Dr. Simmons, the heart specialist who had implanted Duffy's pacemaker, wasn't overjoyed to be called to the hospital in the middle of the night, but was even less overjoyed to hear personnel at the nurse's station talking about a patient's wife and her seemingly odd behavior. He was in the midst of admonishing them about gossip when something popped into his mind. Something he had read recently in a medical journal. He asked to see the offending bracelet and suddenly, the picture became clear to him. Mrs. Duffy's intense concern for her husband's well being now seemed suspect. With the help of nurse Richards, perhaps her concern could be tested.

Morning brought a harried- looking Mrs. Duffy into ICU, immediately asking how her husband had fared during the night. A detective, disguised in hospital scrubs, feigned work in Duffy's room. Mrs. Duffy saw the bracelet laying on the bedside table and as she placed it on his wrist, spoke softly to him, yet loudly enough for the disguised detective to hear. "I don't know why this stuffy old hospital has such stiff rules. I put your bracelet on each day and each day, someone removes is. But we know what sentiment it holds, don't we *dearie?* Only you and your secretary and of course me, know she gave it to you after the *business* trip the two of you went on last month. Too bad you didn't take time to read the pamphlet that came with it. Doesn't it just make your heart flutter to know you are wearing your lover's gift? She will never have you, not even for another business trip."

That was all the detective needed to hear before saying, "Mrs. Duffy, you are under arrest for the attempted murder of your husband."

"That's ridiculous. I come here every possible hour to watch over him. How can you possibly....?"

Her sentence was interrupted as Dr. Simmons entered the room holding a small box in one hand and what looked like a magazine in the other.

"Mrs. Duffy, I heard from the nurses that you kept putting that bracelet on your husband's wrist. It jarred my memory of a recent article in this medical journal. Copper bracelets come with a strong warning that people with heart problems requiring pacemakers should not wear them because them cause the implanted devices to malfunction. You must have found the box your husband's bracelet came in and actually read the pamphlet that came with it. You knew wearing a copper bracelet would sooner or later cause his pacemaker to malfunction and ultimately lead to your husband's death. That is why you kept putting it back on. Too bad so few people are aware of the adverse effect copper has on those modern miracle life savers. Nurse Richards checked just after you left last night to make sure the bracelet wasn't on your husband's arm. You must have slipped back in and returned it to his arm, knowing he was in no shape to know what you were doing."

Mrs. Duffy's outburst surprised them. "That's the way he deserves to die—at the hand of his lover. *She* gave it to him. *She* is the one who was killing him. I was just helping fate along."

A sobbing Mrs. Duffy did not resist as the detective led her away in handcuffs.

ROOF TOP MEETING

Unrelenting heat from the mid-day sun reminded Jim that he'd had nothing to eat since stepping off the ladder onto his A frame roof hours ago. He had carefully nailed strips of wood onto the roof, making temporary safety steps to be used for climbing to the peak of this picturesque cabin. Or so it had appeared when he first viewed it rising majestically above treetops as he walked along the narrow canopied lane a few miles from town. He had needed the solitude as he pondered the next move in his unsettled life.

He sighed and reflected: this is where it all started The Tilghman's Community Center had been severely damaged by fire in 1956. Common sense ruled it a total loss. Several neighboring farmers planned to raze whatever remained of the old structure which had originally been an elementary school but was closed in the late 40s due to lack of enrollment and used as a meeting place for community residents of all ages. After cotton and corn crops were harvested, the men would pool their efforts and clear the building site within a week.

Perhaps luck, perhaps fate, who knows? Rain fell off and on for several days. The demolition project was delayed. During this delay, an adventurous dream was born.

Mason Hall High School's Future Farmers of America (FFA) and the Future Homemakers of America (FHA) requested and received permission to work on the demolition and use the site for future projects which would benefit the community while fitting in with President Roosevelt's reason for creating the FFA and FHA. He felt the Great Depression found Americans unprepared to be self-sufficient and believed as president, it was his responsibility to do whatever he could to encourage independence and self-reliance.

This was Roosevelt country. If he asked, they gave. They believed. They followed. They trusted and worked tirelessly to 'take care of their own.

Ah, memories. It was memories that led Jim to have his attorney purchase the Norton farm nearby and relocate the tenants.

High school boys and girls worked every available hour with teachers and neighbors to clear the site. They heard stories of projects Miss Obera Minton, the spinster teacher who taught 1st through 8th grades in one room instituted such as a bird sanctuary with bird houses and feeders made by students one year. They had heard about the year she and the students had grown their own garden with each student being responsible for one kind of plant. It was this memory as much as Eleanor Roosevelt's Victory Gardens that led students to grow their own Victory Garden, which in their youthful ambition was envisioned as the biggest and best in the state of Tennessee.

The new structure started as a storage shed for equipment and supplies but ended up an almost exact replica of the old Tilghman's School Jim and his classmates had heard their parents talk about.

As Jim sauntered along, occasionally glancing up at that roof peak, he congratulated himself on having seen both his children graduate from universities and secure positions in the world of business.

He could hardly congratulate himself on his marriage however. After almost thirty years, he had been shocked to receive a demand for divorce, a very costly one. His now ex-wife wanted not only half of their assets, she wanted the penthouse in Manhattan, the rustic cabin in Northern Michigan, the country home in Kentucky where she could indulge her love for horses. *Love for horses?* She hated them and that farm and anything connected to it. But her attorney, her trio of them actually, which Jim had paid for, penned pleas that she not be denied her beloved horses. It was easier to just give her what she wanted than to fight.

When he asked why the bitterness, she said, "You have built houses. You have built bridges. You have built shopping plazas, parks, apartment complexes, skyscrapers, glass and chrome penthouses, but you never took time to build a marriage."

Her last demand was that he build her a 'Tea Room' in downtown New York City. YUK!! He couldn't stand the stuff.

He had complied with all her demands, retreated to his roots where he realized he first developed his love for building, bought that A frame house he had seen while walking and now, as he began his descent from repairing that steep roof, noticed his ladder had fallen over and was resting against the big Oak that provided shade for his hammock. The previous owners had left a large trampoline which Jim had pushed aside immediately and installed the hammock where he had already spent many hours even though he had not officially moved into the house.

Short of jumping thirty feet to the ground and probably breaking one or both legs, there was no way down. By climbing higher, he might try leaping to a branch of the Oak but if he missed, injuries would undoubtedly be more than broken legs.

He sat in the blazing sun, feet securely planted on the supports he had installed on his way up. A highly successful architect whose work had been featured in several trade magazines, he had received safety awards based on low percentage of injuries while constructing complicated projects. He had drilled safety into the brains of every employee, especially supervisors. Now, here he was, alone and stranded.

As Jim pondered his plight, he heard a clear voice belting out *Hello Dolly*. No one was in sight. This lane was home to only one other house; a small gingerbread style cottage complete with white picket fencing and a two seater swing hanging from the ceiling of a wrap-around porch.

He knew the spinster librarian for the Rutherford Library lived there with her dog and an assortment of cats. He had seen her when checking out a few books. She wore dresses buttoned up to her neck, hair in a severe bun and tortoise shell framed glasses.

Who could that be singing? He owned all of the land surrounding this retreat except the one acre occupied by the gingerbread house.

Calling for help seemed to be his only option. "Hello!" The singing stopped momentarily and then began again at a lower volume.

"Hello down there!" This time, the voice was silenced and within a few minutes, he saw a woman with long wavy hair floating around her shoulders as the breeze tickled the atmosphere. Pink cheeks topped a partially unbuttoned shirtwaist dress above bare feet. From one hand dangled a pair of sensible oxfords.

"Well hello", she said cautiously, as she peered from behind a clump of honeysuckle vines that had overtaken the mail box and climbed several feet of the split rail fence along his driveway. "Do you need assistance?"

"Do I need assistance? Damm it woman! Do you think I 'm sitting up here sunning myself?"

She laughed. Laughed! Laughed at him!

"Why you".........were the only words he had time to utter as the piece of wood his heel was braced on began sliding.

"The ladder," he yelled, but it was too late. The woman responded with hardly a thought by pushing the trampoline to the spot she thought he would land. Land he did!. He hit it like an expert marksman hits a bulls eye. Suddenly, he was at least twenty feet in the air with no idea how to stop bounding.

She was still laughing. Several minutes later, he was flat on his back on the trampoline with no injuries other than trampled pride.

"Are you all right   Sorry I laughed but you looked so funny."

"Funny? You'll think funny! Who are you anyway? And what are you doing on my property?"

By now, she had buttoned her dress back up to her collar and was unsuccessfully trying to tame her mane.

"Oh. I'm really sorry. I'm Miss Johnstone and I am your neighbor. I wasn't trying to spy. I only wanted to see what you were doing to this beautiful home and until you yelled, I had no idea you were here."

"As you can see, I'm here, for better or worse."

"You took quiet a tumble. Here, let me help you off that trampoline. Lucky for you the previous owner abandoned it. They had teenage sons who were actually quite good with it."

"Let me make you a cup of tea and get something on that sunburn or you'll be very uncomfortable in a few hours."

"I don't like tea and don't have anything in the house except a bag of take out from the deli in town and a couple of cans of pop. I'm not living here yet. I have a room at the Kenton House and just come out here for a few hours each day."

"Then come down to my humble abode and I will make you some tea and rub some aloe on your sunburn."

"Look. I'm not a child. I'm a man and you have no idea who I am. Are you always so careless with your personal safety?"

"Of course I know who you are. We went to Tilghman's together, then to Mason Hal and even worked on the Tilghman's Community Center project together. You're Jim and I'm Nancy."

"Nancy? Nancy Beard? I thought the librarian lived here."

"I am the librarian, Jim. Oh, I get it. My hair. My glasses. I went to college after graduation. Remember you were a year ahead of me? I earned a degree in Literature but ended up working as a librarian in Detroit for years before seeing an ad in the Tri-City reporter seeking a mature librarian. For some reason, that re-awakened a need for home. My grandmother had left this little house to me and I dreamed of someday living here. I answered the ad by email as directed, made an appointment for an in person interview and 'matured' myself a bit. Mature they wanted. Mature they got. But, when I leave the library and come home, I revert to the barefoot, pig-tailed girl who loved to visit Grandmother and run down this beautiful lane."

They had walked as they talked and he now sat in the swing on the porch. She had brought him a cup of tea, broken a spear off her Aloe plant and rubbed the cool soothing gel-like substance over his shoulders and back. The calming effect of her hands slowly gliding over his burning skin was almost mesmerizing. His mind wandered back to the months he had worked on that long ago high school project.

Suddenly, it was he who was laughing. He was remembering another time when Nancy's hands had touched him although not in this tender, healing way. The community center project had been hard work but as teenagers will do, they found ways to squeeze in some fun. He had been raking piles of debris to be burned when he saw a small garden variety snake. She ran. He chased. They ended in a tangle of flailing limbs, snake long dropped, but knowing that, Nancy retaliated by pushing him to the ground, sitting on top of him, pinning his arms to the ground. He should have known that with four brothers, she was not to be teased without consequences.

Alas. By morning, both realized they had been rolling around in Poison Ivy. Both had red, itchy hands and he had an itchy rash on his back and shoulders as well. Yuk! He could still recall his mother's remedy: a paste made by mixing soda and lard. It stung like mad and was messy, but effective.

Apparently, she also was remembering the incident. Both Jim and Nancy collapsed on the cushions of her porch swing, laughing like teenagers again. It was as if time had stood still and they were again dreaming of their future as they had during high school years, planning to go *somewhere*. Well, they had both been somewhere, both returned to their roots and now, both were happily recalling those carefree days of their youth when the entire world was theirs to conquer. Both had conquered a corner of the world, found it somehow lacking and now, had returned to conquer that feeling of being home.

The pot of tea had been abandoned. When laughter allowed, Nancy took the pot of tea inside to reheat it.

Jim decided he probably did like tea after all.

TEA ANYONE?

Above his hospital bed was a sign which read *keep feet elevated 10 degrees.* Registered nurse, Renee Blanchard, knew the almost lifeless body belonged to Richard Wilson. Even so, she followed hospital procedure and checked the plastic wristband hanging loosely around his bony arm which lay atop the sheet worn thin from repeated bleaching, making his weight loss obvious. Below his name, other information included a date of admission twenty-two days ago. Checking his heart rate, she noted on the chart 44 beats per minute, weak and irregular. Barely more than half the number she would have been recording for a healthy man. She also checked his feet and ankles for swelling. And, not for the first time, she activated the button that raised his feet and wondered which nurse had failed to follow that instruction.

Wilson had been rolled into ICU three weeks ago, transported from St. John's emergency room following a heart attack—non-responsive, face ashen, cold, clammy skin.

As she checked the five other patients in the intensive care unit, her mind wandered over the time Wilson had been in her unit. His Dr. had instructed nurses and aides to keep his feet slightly elevated. He was receiving nutrition by way of a feeding tube inserted in his stomach. Despite having the hospital's best heart specialist and receiving medication that should have rendered some improvement, no change was seen.

She wondered if she should chance causing a problem for some other nurse if she mentioned that the bed had not always been elevated. It could have been accidentally done by anyone but the nurses were trained to watch for those mishaps. Reluctant to create an issue with fellow workers, she made a mental note to pay special attention to this patient.

His weeping wife, Helen, was beside his side as he was wheeled into ICU those three weeks ago and she had stayed with him most of the time, night and day since. She went home for a few hours late each afternoon and returned before the night shift arrived. She said she did not want him to wake up at night when the surroundings were quiet and not know where he was.

Helen held his hand despite the plastic tubing attached to his arm allowing life sustaining liquid to slowly drip into his veins. It kept him hydrated and served as a vehicle for medication since he could not swallow.

Every night, she came bearing two thermoses of hot tea: one for the nurses and one for her to sip while watching her ailing husband's chest rise and fall with every labored breath. Since Helen had told the nurses she had done volunteer work in hospitals for several years, they felt comfortable with her vigil so they checked on him hourly, trusting her to call if a problem arose. She had called for a nurse a few times regarding labored breathing and once, she asked why there were empty IV bags

Nurse Renee continued with her rounds and suddenly, a thought entered her mind. Empty IV bags? *EMPTY IV BAGS!!* Renee recalled one of the supervising nurses asking if anyone had damaged IV bags. She seemed to think her inventory was off.

Renee was an avid mystery reader and sensed one was at hand. She decided to forgo Helen's offer of hot tea the following night. The tea she brought was so soothing the nurses often found themselves relaxed to the point of drowsiness while sitting at the desk doing paper work. Renee alerted an orderly of her vague suspicions and determined to take her own thermos of tea. Spicy ginger should keep her on her toes. She knew hospital rules called for cell phones to be turned off unless on break, but she decided to take a chance just in case she needed to prove her suspicions. Her smart phone took very clear pictures and could even make videos. Ah. The miracle of modern technology. If the wife was doing nothing wrong, Renee might lose her job. On the other hand, if her suspicions had any validity, she might save a life. Questions swam in her head. Due to past experiences, some of her coworkers already called her Miss Agatha (as in Agatha Christy) thinking she looked for suspicious actions when they did not exist. Ok. So her almost obsessive immersion in murder mystery novels made her a target for such teasing. Still.........

Just after midnight, with an orderly outside the door, Renee peeked in Richard's room. Everything seemed normal. Renee started working on records at the desk. Other nurses were doing the same. Renee just could not concentrate on her charting. The patient's wife knew the nurse's schedule for rounds and also was aware that cameras were constantly scanning ICU for safety and images were sent back to screens at the nurse's station. Renee thought that the time nurses were making rounds would be wifey's time to make her move.

Sure enough, at 12:35 A.M. while nurses were at the other end of the hallway, Renee, who had managed to quietly slip into the ICU bathroom, saw Helen Wilson make her move. She aimed the smart phone towards the bed and saw Helen remove an IV bag from its 'tree'.

She then witnessed this devoted wife remove the lid to her thermos. Unable to see clearly all that was being done, she moved a few inches and managed to see Helen put a covered cup of clear liquid into her purse. Even from the distance of several feet and in semi-darkness, Renee could see the IV tube was now slowly introducing amber colored liquid into Richard's veins. Renee rushed forward, quickly pushing Helen away from the bed and at the same time, the orderly, waiting outside, grabbed Helen as she tried to flee. By now, Renee had removed the IV from Richard's arm. Emergency staff speedily worked to discover what was now coursing through Richard's body. Hopefully, they were fast enough to prevent permanent harm.

The orderly and security guard detained Helen until police arrived. She railed at them, yelling that they had no right to hold her. She was just trying to comfort him.

Within a short time, healing water had diluted the erroneously introduced liquid to a safe level and Richard blinked his eyes, showing signs of responsiveness for the first time since admission. She had completely fooled all of the hospital staff as well as attending physicians.

With hospital labs at hand, it was quickly determined that the cup in Helen's purse contained the life sustaining nutrition enhanced saline drawn from the IV tube. The thermos on the bedside table showed traces of arsenic and large amounts of Benadryl and melatonin. No wonder he had been sleeping so much. Either of those over the counter drugs alone would have caused drowsiness and lack of attention. Arsenic would have been causing much more deadly effects and the lab tech suspected she had probably been slowly introducing arsenic for a long time. Minute amounts do not show up in blood work but after this period of time, it had built up to a measurable level. But why?

The thermos of tea at the nurse's station Helen had so generously provided also showed low levels of Benedryl and melatonin, just enough to cause them to feel sleepy and perhaps not at their peak performance.

Sobbing frantically, Helen finally confessed she had been trying to weaken Richard so recovery would be impossible. She didn't really want him to die, just remain in a state of non- responsiveness to give her time to think. Although she and Richard had lived together for many years, they never got married. They had merged bank accounts and jointly owned property but for some reason, he was reluctant to actually get officially married. She feared death would uncover that fact and she would lose the life style she had become accustomed to. She hoped if he stayed in a comatose state, she could ultimately move him to a long term facility and she would have time and opportunity to somehow get financial control of what she believed should rightfully be hers.

Renee commented to other nurses that where Helen was going to be living for a few years, hot tea would probably be a rare treat.

Part III

I claim numerous poems as my handiwork, mostly written about real places or real people. Following are a few that hold special meaning to me.

I share the love of poetry with several friends but especially with three special friends with whom I meet once a month. We challenge ourselves by taking turns choosing a subject to write about. Amazingly, we frequently write about similar thoughts or ideas. I would like to take this opportunity to thank Marilyn, Laurie and Pati for many enjoyable hours spent sharing ideas and feelings. None of us have had professional training in poetry writing but all have produced some great words. As mentioned earlier in my writing, one does not need to be a professional to do something they enjoy. Therefore, I encourage my readers to start putting pen to paper, sharing with friends your thoughts, ideas and feelings.

This poem is about a large Oak that stands in the front yard of the home of one of my sisters in Tennessee farm country.

THE GREAT OAK

It must be nigh on a hundred years since that acorn took its fall.

Since then, it's slowly inched upward, probably a hundred twenty feet tall.

Its roots reach deep into the ground.

Its moss dappled trunk maybe fifteen feet 'round.

Giant branches span out as wide as its tall,
esconed in foliage from spring to fall.
This old tree's home to many a bird;
from early morn 'till dark they can be heard.
A swarm of bees makes its home in a hollow
as the queen bee buzzes 'round, her worker bees follow.
They gather pollen from blossoms nearby.
Then soar back home 'neath the hot summer sky.
This Oak tree provided shade for an old wooden swing
While it stands tall with posture fit for a king.
Ants scamper over the bark, rough and old.
A woodpecker hammers a rat-a-tat-tat so bold.
A mother squirrel scampers quickly to her lofty nest.
She'll give their climbing skills a mother's strict test.
Can they jump limb to limb, scale trees up and down?
Can they run like the wind when their feet hit the ground?
A butterfly soars by, its movement soothing.
A caterpillar lazes on a leaf—just snoozing.
As I sit 'neath the shade
of this great Oak tree.
I wish the whole world
this scene could see.
~MKE

The following poem was written about the home of my my paternal great-grandparents in Iuka, Mississippi. In my living room sets a stone which weighs about fifteen pounds and is from the ruins of the chimney of the old home I am writing about. The house was demolished long ago but a pile of stones still mark the spot where it stood. In order to gain access to this stone, I had to walk out into a field of tall grass and weeds. That is where I got my first and only case of chiggers. My advice to one and all is that unless walking out into such fields is very important, avoid doing so at all costs. For me however, it was important. It was a place the entire family enjoyed visiting once or twice a year during my childhood. You may recall that was many years ago when traveling took much more time. In our Model A, we would leave home long before daylight and could only have a few hours visit in order to get back home the same day. The first time I remember making that trip was when Daddy had just become the owner of that Model A. He did not buy it, rather traded two young calves for it. The barter system worked well in those days. Pa and Ma both lived into their 90s.

THE OLD LOG CABIN

Though old and decaying as I know it was,
That cabin was heaven to me.
Pa and Ma sat on the long shaded porch
barely moving in hand made rocking chairs.
Their aging feet and weakened knees
kept them from descending the stairs
which led to a rich verdant expanse of grass

where they'd strolled as a lad and a lass.
Just very young lovers when they came here to stay
building a happy life as they toiled night and day.
Six children they bore amid hard work and strife,
eking out a living from land tired of giving life.
It was almost a forest—trees crushing all around.
With axe, saw and shovel, they cleared some ground.
Just enough space for a family to live,
to grow a garden, to take and to give.
They built this cabin with their very own hands
with timber hewn from trees on their lands.
First, just two rooms, then over the years
More rooms were added 'mid laughter and tears.
The garden grew larger, more acres were seeded.
More land was cleared as more space was needed.
The kids are all grown; time has taken it toll.
Just a pile of old rubble is left on that knoll.
But a big sturdy Oak still looks toward the sky
as traffic on the new road steadily speeds by.
The spirits of Ma and Pa still dwell in the land
where their dearly loved log cabin used to stand
~MKE

The following poem was written about an old weather beaten barn that sets on a farm across from the country home of another of my sisters in Tennessee.

THE OLD BARN

Ah……the stories this old barn could tell.

It's known several families over the year so well.

It was home for the animals used on the farm,

sheltered them through storms and kept them from harm.

The hay loft a haven for children to play,

climbing the ladder to jump down in loose hay.

Sturdy bales of hay would be stacked to the peak,

A perfect place for kids playing hide and seek.

On a rainy day with no outside work to do,

a great place to retreat with a book or two.

a glass of iced tea and an old a blanket for ease

with the loft door open to let in the breeze.

A quiet place to just let the mind restfully wander

or if troubled, a peaceful spot to sit and ponder.

Years have gone by, only the home site remains.

What was once a family farm, now leased to strangers as progress gains.

But this rusty old barn still stands in its place,

probably hoping for a familiar face.

One riding horse now makes the barn its abode.

He can frolic and graze in a spot by the road.

Still this withered old barn vows to stand fast
Happily recalling memories from the long ago past.
~MKE

This next poem was written about a house that still stands in Keego Harbor, Michigan. It is one of only a few left intact after the state purchased property and demolished buildings in order to widen and straighten about a mile of twisting road.

PROGRESS
He sits on the porch of the little white house
   and rocks back and forth every day.
He watches the traffic, the boats and the cars
   as people rush into the fray.
Fifty years back, when just a young man
   he staked his claim on this place.
Fifty years of work, toil, trouble and pain
   have left maps of time on his face.
This little white house, across from the lake,
   he built with his own steady hand,
When man was known by the sweat of his brow
   and the love he had for the land.
This little plot, just 60x80, he called his very own soil.
He dreamed, saved, laughed, worked, but he never
   minded the toil.

The basement, the floors, the walls, then the roof
   and finally, his dream home was done.
But there was something else he needed—a mate
   and he knew just the one.
So, he married his Jenny and took her home
     to his little white house near the lake.
They loved, they prospered, they had two sons.
   His dream home was not a mistake.
Now his boys have grown up and have their own life.
   His Jenny has faded away.
But he still has his little white house
   where he can sit quietly and pray.
Now, progress, prosperity, and a need for more homes
   has encroached upon his space.
Big houses, bigger houses, stones, mortar and brick
   Have been built all around his place.
The trees he planted when first he came
   have now grown very tall.
While the road has been widened and widened again
   'til his front yard is now very small.
 Still, he sits on the porch of his little white house,
   four rooms, a dog and a cat.
He is old now, worried, watching the world's rush,
   just sitting there with his pipe and his hat.
He knows it's just a matter of time

until *they* offer him one of their deals.
Sell his house? Leave his home?
   Do they know, even care how he feels?
Across the street and down the road
   many of the old houses are gone.
Still, he sits on the porch and vows he'll stay
   even though he may soon be alone.
The paint is peeling, the posts are leaning
   and the porch has a bit of a slope.
Hours, days, weeks and years.
   Time has passed at a lope.
If this be progress, and it is, so they say.
   Of it, he surely wants none.
He's getting on now, a bit slow, not young anymore.
   Just wants his place in the sun.
So he sits on the porch of his little white house
   and watches progress…. Progress.
~MKE

    This poem is about another house which actually exists, a very small house which meets no current codes but due to the 'grandfather' clause, can still be occupied.

THE LITTLE BLUE HOUSE

Just a little blue house, white window frames,
white door.

If the city had its way, it would be there
no more.
For one thing, the paint must have been bought
on sale.
It wasn't meant for painting homes, you can
easily tell.
Its too bright by far for the newer sedate
neighborhood.
where houses, not homes, all look like duplicates.
It's just understood.
I've never been inside this colorful
tiny frame.
I don't even know the occupant's
full name.
Neighbors call her "Grans". She's just always
been there.
But the city doesn't like her house; they seem not
to care.
It doesn't fit into the bigger plans
they've made;
the zone, the rules, the drawings
they've laid.
The rooms must be tiny, probably
just two.
But the front room has a big window with

an outside view.
She wakes every morning and pulls
her shade.
She has no plans or schedules that
need to be made.
Except how to keep her little
blue home.
A stranger might think it is occupied by
a gnome.
When the city first told her the house was
too old.
The neighbors joined forces and gave it
an uplift.
Now, the city can call meetings and sit down
to sift
through papers, zonings, rules
for ways
to tell Grams she should start counting
her days.
She sits by her window, her gray hair a
neat bun.
Watching school kids as they play
and run.
She gives them warm, spicy gingerbread men.

But the house is too small to invite
them in.
They sit on her front porch, just a bit of
crooked board s,
while people from the new subdivision look down on her
like lords.
She's lived in this house nigh on
seventy years,
built when homes were constructed with hard work,
sweat and tears..
As she now wipes unashamed tears on
her sleeve,
she vows she'll die
before she
will leave.
~MKE

    The following poem is written about a much loved site in rural Tennessee, occupied by a woman in her late 80s. She had lived in that home since her very young years. As she aged and her health began failing, she let her children know she wanted them to allow her to die in this home rather than placing her in what they considered a safer and more convenient location. She was able to take care of her basic needs with the help of one of my sisters who ran errands for her and took her for necessary shopping and doctor appointments. She was able to stay in her Corner of Paradise until a few weeks before her time on earth ended.

HER CORNER OF PARADISE

In a swing 'neath the Silver Birch tree

is where she loves to be.

The tree top reaches skyward almost as high

as the eye can see.

Surrounded by nature, mostly untouched by human hand.

Within her vision, acres of lush farm land.

The home site which is actually quiet small

has been made into a haven for family and woodland creatures all.

Coral roses, purple flox, and tiger lilies galore.

Circling the lawn are brilliant black-eyed susans and more,

There's a bird bath complete with a hand painted red bird.

Yet, in the twilight, real bird song can be heard.

Her ceramic ducks are sunning beneath lilacs full grown.

Ah---the loving care this garden has known.

Her hands that were so supple

in the long ago past

are now gnarled, often swollen,

and proudly wear age lines.

She's lived in this little house for many a year.

She often and openly will shed a tear

For the good times, the sad times
and all in between.
For the bountiful, wondrous life she has seen.
In this corner of paradise she calls her own.
Never can she imagine any other home.
~MKE

Books have been a big part of my life as far back as I can remember. My mother sometimes scolded me because she would find me reading a book instead of doing what I was supposed to. I cannot imagine not being surrounded by books and still will read most anything printed and confess to having frequently ignored important things such as laundry, cooking or cleaning in order to 'finish just this one chapter'. My husband and I had many unfriendly 'discussions' regarding my habit of staying up until the wee hours to finish a book.

BOOKS

I open the covers of a brand new book

and what do you think I see?

Words, phrases and sentences galore

surely penned just for me.

My fingertips hover over rich parchment

as reverently I turn crisp pages.

I wonder with dazzling awe if they have been

labored over by long ago sages.

The thoughts and ideas are new to me but surely must be very old.

They simply continue telling tales from our past
as history has always been told.
Are there really any glorious stories unwritten?
Writers have always told of young lovers smitten.
Wars and wars and rumors of war have filled pages and pages of texts.
When all has been written about wars and love
then what can be thought of next?
You can breathe words and dreams about how they look
tumbled across pages of a much loved book.
Colors become vivid, emotions alive with the sweep of an ink-dipped pen.
One writes of nature, of good and evil,
perhaps of sinners and sin.
If we read only of the shining and good, does it tell the entire story of life?
Would it picture the work and sadness and tears,
tell of unending strife?
Would it recall the sweat, heartaches, days and nights spent at labor
sharing of time, both good and sad,
spent with close friend and neighbor?
Books may entice you to fantasy, to imagination,
to dreams.
They make you wonder if all is as it seems.
As I open this book—this much loved book—my mind wanders a bit

over ideas , philosophies, history, loves and thoughts which make me want to never close it.
~MKE

    I was well into adulthood before I entered the world of book clubs. At one time, I was participating in three but found after reading all of the selections, I had little time to read books of my own choosing. I am now in only one and thoroughly enjoy the monthly group discussions. It stretches my choice of reading and causes me to read books I otherwise would not choose. Hurray for book clubs.

BOOK CLUBS
My Book club help keep my brain in gear.
Reading, fantasying, imagining, makes my thinking clear.
There are biographies, histories and love stories sweet.
When a handsome, dashing prince sweeps me off my feet.
There's murder, mayhem, mystery. Oh My!
They make me think like a private eye.
There's Grisham, Baldachi, and Evanovich.
I like them all, but what to read? Which?
Once a month readers meet in a group.
Through the library shelves we search as a troup.
Monday afternoon's selections are chosen.

Sometimes my list goes to more than a dozen.

Which one to use as our main discussion?

Pen and paper in hand,

I'm now on a mission.

We must choose just one—what a gigantic task.

Why is that so difficult, you might well ask.

But with Pati, Jenny, Margaret and Flo,

you can't just pick up one book and go.

Laurie, Mary, Marilyn, and Sue.

feverently use their book sharpened thought

trying to find out what new book you have brought.

Was it a Danielle Steele, a Sandra Brown or maybe a Grafton, Sue?

All those authors. Which one appeals to you?

James Patterson? Ken Follett? Ralph Nader or Carolyn Keene?

Debbie MaComber? Lisa Wingate? Jim Fergus? It remains to be seen.

Mary Higgins Clark, Agatha Christie, Beverly Lewis to name a few.

Earl Stanley Gardner, Nathaniel Hawthorne, and another name or two.

So, hurray for book clubs. May they always be,

bringing sanity, comedy and enlightenment to me.

~MKE

Thanks for reading my book. I sincerely hope you enjoyed it and found at least one bit of helpful information.

If you would like to contact me, you may do so at pubauthor2015@gmail.com

I would appreciate your comments.